About the Author

During the fabled fifties, PORTIA NELSON'S singing was the toast of Cafe Society in New York City and in other cities of the world. She is a Renaissance Lady who is also a composer, lyricist, arranger, painter, photographer and actress who is currently seen in the Television Soap Opera, ALL MY CHILDREN, as Mrs. Gurney. She has also been in such films as THE SOUND OF MUSIC, DR. DOLITTLE, THE TROUBLE WITH ANGELS, THE OTHER, and on Broadway in the award-winning THE GOLDEN APPLE. She has written music and lyrics for many revues, television specials and films. She arranged and composed a tongue-in-cheek rock album (instrumental), LADY NELSON AND THE LORDS. As a singer, she has recorded five show albums for Columbia Records and three solo albums. Most recently, she formed a unique, intimate musical of this book, THERE'S A HOLE IN MY SIDEWALK, which played at the York Theatre in Manhattan. She directed, wrote music and lyrics and performed in the production.

Personal Note

I choose to call these thoughts "pieces"...pieces of me. These pieces have had a bit of trouble finding a comfortable concept that would knit them into one book...just as I have had difficulty molding a multi-faceted misfit into one person.

More than anything, they are evidence, to me, that here in the middle of my life I have finally gained a small pinpoint of self-awareness...false images stripped away... "through a glass darkly, but, now...face to face." No hiding, anymore, behind innocence and ignorance.

It isn't necessarily easier, now...but I have a self that I trust and the feelings in the experiences are mine...not what I *should* feel...not what I was taught to feel and not something someone else felt that I admired and imitated. Knowing one's own feelings and being able to trust them is the difference between existing and living. So, that's what I have here, I guess...living and loving experiences...pieces of my small universe that can, I hope, be recognized by yours.

THERE'S A HOLE IN MY SIDEWALK

BY PORTIA NELSON

To Susan & Meyer —
From Denny's
special friend
Portia

STONEBARN PUBLISHING ● LOS ANGELES

STONEBARN EDITION
November, 1988
© 1977, Portia Nelson

ISBN: 0-9621159-0-8 (previously published under ISBN 0-445-03199-9)

This book is available at a discount in large quantities. Have your organization or special-interest group contact

Stonebarn Publishing
13601 Ve...
Suite 345
Sherman Oaks, Calif. 91423

*"I am a part of all
that I have met."*
Tennyson

*To all of you,
whoever you are,
I, humbly, dedicate
this book.*

CONTENTS

A story of
Me in You
and
You in Me
in
Four Parts

PROLOGUE

I know you, by me . . . .
        and me, by you.
A mirrored exchange
        of awareness . . . loving.
        Loving awareness . . .
            Always becoming . . .
            becoming always
            more you in me
            and me in you . . . .
Growing separately together . . . .
changing and remaining the same
        eternally.

Part One

My life has been a series
        of wonderful experiences.
It's a pity I wasn't there
        for most of them.

THERE'S A HOLE IN MY SIDEWALK

*Autobiography
in
Five Short Chapters*

I

I walk down the street.
> There is a deep hole in the sidewalk.
> I fall in.
> I am lost…I am helpless.
>> It isn't my fault.

It takes forever to find a way out.

II

I walk down the same street.
> There is a deep hole in the sidewalk.
> I pretend I don't see it.
> I fall in again.

I can't believe I am in this same place.
>> But, it isn't my fault.

It still takes a long time to get out.

III

I walk down the same street.
> There is a deep hole in the sidewalk.
> I *see* it is there.
> I still fall in...it's a habit...but,
>> my eyes are open.
>> I know where I am.
>
> It is *my* fault.
> I get out immediately.

IV

I walk down the same street.
> There is a deep hole in the sidewalk.
> I walk around it.

V

I walk down another street.

I don't know what I want, sometimes,
  But I know
  that I want to know
  what I want.
I know that once I know what I want
  I will be able to get it.
Of course, I may not want what I get
  when I get it . . . .
But, at least,
  I'll know I don't want that!
Then, I can move on to something else
  I don't know if I want.
    That's progress!

You say you love me for who I am . . . .
But . . .
who you think I am
                is not *who* I am.
Therefore,
it's hard for me to be who I am
                when we're together . . .
because . . .
I think I have to be
                who you think I am.

Of course,
I don't know exactly who it is
                you think I am . . .
I just know it isn't who I am.

Who am I?
Well . . . .
Who I am is something I recognize
when someone tells me
who I am *not*.
At least, I *think* that's *not* who I am.
Maybe who I am *not*
                is who I *am*!
If that's who I am . . . . MY GAWD . . .
                you really love me.

I used to suffer a great deal
thinking I was the only one
        in the world
        so lonely
        and troubled.

Then, I opened the door to myself
and discovered there were
        millions
        of people
        just like me.

It isn't lonely anymore . . . .
but it's miserable to be
        so ordinary.

I know why we are friends.
It's because I don't always
                approve of you.

You don't think you deserve approval,
So . . . . if I gave it to you
                you would not
                approve of me
and I would lose your trust.

Friendship is based on trust
                and I want you
                to trust me
because I need your approval.

However, if I get your approval
                I will not trust you
because I don't think I deserve approval,
                either.

I know why we are friends.

You want to please me . . . and,

I want to please you . . . .

      so please make the decision
      about where we are going tonight.

If *I* make the decision . . .
      and then *you* don't like it,
      you'll be mad at me
      and I'll be miserable all evening
      because I haven't pleased you.

Now . . . if *you* try to please me . . . .
      and *you* make the decision,
      if *I* don't like it
      when we get there . . . .
      at least, *you* will be pleased.

If I am unhappy with where we are,
      or what we are doing,
      that's allright . . . . . .

because it won't be my decision
that will have made me unhappy.
      It will be yours.
      Therefore,
      it will be *your* fault!
            That will please me.

You say you will never leave me
      because I understand you.
And I love being thought of
      as "understanding".

But, I also understand
      that by being so understanding,
      you automatically
      have the freedom
      to do as you please . . . .
      because . . . . .
if I am not understanding,
      you will leave me.

I think that what I really
      have to understand is this:
In order to be so understanding all the time,
      (so that you will not leave me),
      I have to leave myself.
If I am not myself
      when I am being so understanding,
      who the hell is it
      you will never leave?

Better I should not be so understanding
      so there's somebody
      you can leave.

You have made a fool of me!

I know I am not the most beautiful,
the most talented, the most intelligent
person in the world. . . .
but I liked you. . . . .
and I wanted you
to think I was.
So. . . . . . .I tried to be beautiful
talented and intelligent
for you.

However,
since I succeeded
in making you believe it,
naturally,
I immediately
lost respect for you
for not seeing
that I had fooled you.

Now . . . . . .
I am intelligent enough,
beautiful enough and
talented enough
not to be associated with fools . . . .
and I am incensed that I didn't see
how foolish you were
at once.
But . . . . . .
I liked you then . . . and . . .
it drove me to make you believe
what I wanted you to believe . . . .

Except.....
        I was so convincing,
        I began to believe it myself!

Now.......
        anybody who believes
        things like that about me
                is a fool.

That makes me a fool!

And if it weren't for you
        believing what I wanted you to,
        I wouldn't know that.

I hate you for making a fool of me!

Will you please stop trying to
              finish my sentences before I do?

It's humiliating!

After all . . . . it is my sentence!
              Let me show it off!

I know you are really trying to let me know
              how sensitive and smart you are . . .
              and how deeply you understand me . . .

But . . . . . . if you are that smart . . . . .
              please let me think that
              I am smarter than you
              by not impressing me with
              how smart you are
              in the middle of my sentences!!!

Of course,
              if I am smart enough
              to be that aware of
              what you are up to . . .
Then,
              I should be smart enough to know
              it doesn't matter what you do
              in the middle of my sentences.

Maybe I'm not so smart!

Now, that *is* humiliating!

I want you to love me...

> but I am aware
> that you only love
> what you cannot get.

> So, I can't let you know
> that I am interested
> or you won't love me back.

Now...

> I hate games
> and dishonesty
> more than anything.

Therefore.....

> if I love you enough
> to be dishonest....
> to play a game
> in order to keep you interested,

>> I will hate myself.

> If I hate myself,

>> eventually,
>> I will crack up!

If I crack up.......

> at least,
> you won't be able to get me...

>> because I won't care...
>> or be aware
>> that you even exist....

> and then,
> maybe you will love me.

Jesus! There's got to be a simpler way!

You are strong . . . vital . . .

       very much in control of yourself.

I admire that!

I know you can help me . . .

       and I need help.

But:

       if I allow you to help me,

       I will have to trust you enough

       to give up my own self control.

If I give that up

       I will begin to feel powerless . . .

       without identity . . .

       like a nobody!

How dare you help me to be a nobody!

I cannot seem to leave you . . .
  though often,
  I think I should because
  even though I care . . .
I am not in love with you.
But I am in love with the fact
  that you are in love with me.
It makes me think very well of myself.
When I think well of myself
  I am very nice . . .
  and very creative.
That makes me feel worthwhile and then
  I love myself.
The more I love myself . . .
  the more you love me.
No wonder I can't leave.
  I wouldn't know
  I loved myself . . . .
  without you.

I would like to be one....
A one not worried about being two!
I am more one
        when we are three.
When we are two
        I become zero.
I become zero because
I am afraid you will see
        that I am not one.
When we are three I am comfortable...
It doesn't matter if I am not one
        since I seem to become one
        simply because
        there are two being two
        and letting me be one.
Therefore, I am not zero...I can't be...
Two from three is always one.
So, I am more one when we are three....
        as long as I don't worry about
            being two.

In the beginning,
  everywhere I went,
  I didn't always go along.
I didn't know it then,
  but I was afraid I'd meet myself.
When we finally met,
I wasn't who I expected I'd be . . . .
  but, oh, it was a relief
  to have someone to be with . . .
    at last.

Part Two

I am a hopeless romantic
              who does not believe
              love solves everything.
Still, I weep for the loss
                   of illusion . . . .
              knowing full well
                   that reality
              is unbearable . . . .
without a few gilded window frames
              to see through.

How brazen you are!

You lean across the table . . .
        slender hands
        cupping your face . . .

and stare arrow straight
        into my eyes . . . .
        no blinking at all.

You know you are making a frame

for a remarkably beautiful face.

I stare back . . . .
        not out of desire
        or challenge . . . . .

        but, as my only defense
        against your discovering

how deeply I am immersed in pleasure.

I hope that what you are after
is an exchange . . .
not
a reaction.

One step forward
      into the bright of loving.
Yet, I fear the bright will not last.
      ... so, one step back.
Still, I fear, more,
      the dark of not loving at all.
Well, then ....
      may I take a giant step?
      May I?
I have already answered.
      Shall we dance?

I know who you are.

You are so much of me
        that if I don't love you
        I won't exist.

And I'm selfish.
        I don't want to miss anything.

Two days ago
I never would have believed
I would spring from my bed
        at the first glimmer
                of sunlight . . . .
and drive all over town
        looking for
        blue Volkswagens!

Dear one . . . .

Kind one . . . .

       lend me your dreams
       for a while.

Cover me
       with the sweet sleep
       of your innocence,
and wake me
       with the crystal sunshine
       of your hope.

Light my darkness with fireflies
       and build me air castles
       to house
       the velvet summers
       of love.

Stay with me,
       dear one . . . .
stay with me long enough
       to let me hear, again,
       that far away music
       of yesterday . . .
              when I was young.

Your hair is like a Monk's cap
        made of wheat.

It often slips down over your eyes
        so I can't see if you are
        hiding from me
        or spying on me.

Sometimes,
        I reach out . . . .
        as an artist might . . . .
and make a gentle brush stroke
        on the canvas of your brow
        to change the shape of your cap.

As much as I love it,
I cannot bear to talk to you
        without watching your eyes.

Besides,
        there is such selfish pleasure
        in the act of touching,
        lightly . . .
        hardly at all . . .
making a graceful arc there
and seeing you smile . . .
        as if your hair were attached
        to the corners of your mouth.

There is so much about me that I don't know
until I talk to you.

That first day . . . .

as you turned to leave . . .

we touched . . . .

and, like magnets, we clung to one another

for a long time.

Nothing more.

Yet . . . in that rare moment of holding you

I experienced what I have come to value most . . .

the ecstasy

of

not doing anything

about it.

How wise of you to wait....
to fill the shy, awkward spaces
     with white wine
     and cushioned conversation.
I am aware that you are
     allowing me time
     to become accustomed
to the cities of your smile...
and to window shop your eyes...
     until at last,
     I am so full of you,
that I no longer blush
     on my way into your arms.

Water, Air, Earth, Fire.

Mix together, slowly,
              with ceiling seagulls
              and pear wine.

Stir until the perfect blend . . .

Cool for a moment . . . then,
              place in the fruitful womb
              of love
              to be born again
              into a circle of light . . .

an enchanted world where only believers
              are allowed to enter.

I can feel my fears beginning
                    to settle inside me ..
                    like sleepy kittens
                    upon the hearth.
Shshshsh . . . tip toe . . .
Don't slam doors in my mind . . .
                    not now.
Let the kittens sleep a little while
                    please . . . .
The fire will die soon enough, anyway . . .
And now, while the world is warm . . .
                    hold me.

I think I just fell into a hole
in the sidewalk.

I have said, "I love you"...
        before you,
        and meant it.

Yet,
I would have to admit...
        that laid on the scales,
        the pain of loving
        has often outweighed the joy.

But, it never ceases to amaze me
        that I never died of love.

Looking back....
        knowing I survived...
        pain has become my faith.

Though I am fragile...
        it is my strength.

So, I warn you...
        I will not die of you.

I know that pain and joy
        cannot be separated...
        and, like tomorrow and today
        they become one another.

And so, I remember those
        before you,
and rejoice that I said,
        "I love you,"
        before you....

because,
it will help me not to die of you....
        like I didn't,
        before you.

I am always a grumbling sleepwalker
             in the mornings.

Do you realize . . . .
             for three days in a row
             I have laughed
at least ten times
             before coffee?

It's a dreary day . . . .
Let's just stay inside.
We can pretend that
       Kisses are brushes
       and that we are
       each other's canvas'.
We won't need a northern light . . .
       or any light at all,
       for that matter . . . .
And who cares if we ever finish
       the picture, anyway.

Sorry I didn't answer.
I was listening
    to what you weren't saying.

You are the oldest young person
I have ever known.
It makes me feel younger than you are.
That's a neat trick!

I am so free with you
I never wish to be
    free of you.

The beautiful togetherness
        of our silence
        makes me wonder
why we ever bothered
        to speak at all.

I didn't really
        leave my heart
        in San Francisco...
although I said I did...
But, I certainly
        let it out
        into the fresh
                morning air
and ran it up and down
                a few hills.
I did let it rest
        in the smile
of a beautiful stranger
        for a few days...
But then,
        I snatched it away
        and brought it home
                to you...
as I knew I would
        before I went away
        to be mad at you.

I think I love you most
  in those early hours
  just before sunrise
When,
  spent with loving
  and lost in dreaming,
You reach out,
  like the morning glory vine,
  and wind about
  braiding limb to limb . . .
    binding me to you
    with the tender quiet
    of us.
Desire is buried in slumber . . . .
and,
  asking nothing . . . . .
  giving all . . . .
You bend to touch me
  through a thousand years of knowing
  . . . . . without knowing.
But I know.
I'm glad I'm a light sleeper.

When I listen
        to your feelings,
        and can feel
        your listenings . . .
Only then
        can I expect you
        to hear me.

We are not "in love" . . .
but, we are love.

        I'm glad.

        It lasts longer.

My longing is burning a hole
       in my patience . . .
       time is spinning away.
What good is sleep
       when an eternity
       is rushing by
       that I could be kissing you.
Damn it!
Will you please wake up?
I think I'll turn over . . .
       a little bump
       never hurt anybody!
"Hey! . . . . awake so early?
       I love you."

Please understand . . . .
There are days I must leave you . . .
    in order to be closer to you.
Up close, I cannot search out
    those fragments of you
    that your image of yourself
    hides from me.
At a distance . . .
    uncluttered by sensation . . .
    I can really see you, freely, . . .
    and discover pieces of myself,
        as well.
And then, we come home together . . . . .
    to love you all the more.

You said you didn't love me,
                    this morning.
I didn't believe you.
I knew you just hated yourself.
                    That's allright.
I don't love you, either . . . .
                    today.

Please . . . . . .
don't extract promises from me
that must race quickly
        from the present
        into the past
casting dark shadows on the future.
Now . . . today . . . is all
        we can be certain of
        and love
        is something better
than a collection of pretty vows
to cling to on a rainy day.
What we already are
        is what we will be
                together.
        Isn't that enough?

Stop looking at me like that!
Can't you see how much
    I need you to believe
    what I am saying
So that I can believe it
        myself?

I would give you everything . . .
                    if I could . . . but,
The only gift worth giving
                    is freedom . . . .
the freedom to grow . . .
                    away from me,
                    if necessary.
Of course, one can't give freedom,
but, at least, I know that.
Maybe that's the gift, then . . .
                    the knowing . . . .
And I couldn't tie a ribbon around it
                    even if I wanted to.

Ask something of me . . . .
                please . . .
I know there is no answer . . .
                but often,
I need to feel it would be me
                you would ask,
if there was one.

I am not locking you out!
I am trying very hard
    not to lock you in!
Maybe it's the same thing.

What you seek is my approval . . . . .
　　　　not my self.
So, it is more friendly
　　　　that I turn you
　　　　back to yourself . . .
　　　　the source
　　　　of acceptance.
When you no longer need
　　　　my approval . . . . .
I can give it to you.

You say you love me
        because I understand you
        better than you understand
                yourself.
Sometimes, like now,
        I wish I didn't
        because it forces me to see
        that it is also the reason
        you will have to
                leave me.

You slept on your own side of the bed
                last night...
It was a universe wide.
When I reached out to touch you
              all I could feel
              was the distance
              between.
It is still there today.
Your eyes...that soft bed of blue...
              once my resting place...
are crowded with distant mountains
              and racing rivers.
And I'll be alone...
              with you...
              again, tonight.

This is no carnival!
        I can ride with you . . . .
        but,
        I am not
        your
        merry-go-round.
When you have discovered
        the difference . . . . .
I'll meet you at the Ferris wheel.

I don't smoke . . . .

 so . . . . .

I never thought
          I would miss the stale smell
          of your bent,
          charred cigarettes
          on my bedside table.

          But,

          the clean ashtray
          was as glaring
          as a headlight,
          last night.

          I couldn't sleep.

If I smoked . . . .

          maybe I wouldn't have noticed
          you were gone.

          Maybe.

Let me be angry . . .
please . .
It is the only way
I can keep you from seeing
how much
I need you.

If I say "no" to you

        I will lose you.

If I say "yes" . . . .

        I will lose myself.

Even if I win, I lose.

        Or do I?

I am not a piece of jewelry
        to be worn
        so that others will admire you.
If you choose to continue . . . . .
        you must also remember
        that when jewelry is displayed
        . . . . it can be stolen.

Will you try . . . . just once,
           to be my age?
I'm tired of
           trying to be yours.
Stand up.
Let go of my hand.
Maybe, then . . .
           I can let go of yours.
           You, first.

I know you heard me . . . . .

        but, were you listening?   .

Better stop it now,
       before smiles become tightropes
       for words that step . . .
       with measured coolness . . . .
across mechanical lips into deaf ears.

Please get the hell out of my life . . . .

       only . . . . .

       go softly . . . .

       and don't let me see you go . . .

or I may call you back . . . .

       and there is no one home.

Wait!
You can't leave me now.
What will I do with all these
OREO cookies?

I warn you . . . I will not die of you.

I warn you . . . I will not die of you.

The silence is so loud
    I cannot hear my own advice.

Love, love . . . where are you?
You, alone, soothe the ache . . . .
 and I cannot believe in you.

Today . . .
I know how lonely I am
        for you.
I have mistakenly called
        four people
        by your name.

The most I can hope for,
right now,
is to make it to tomorrow ...
just once ....
without listening
for the phone.

I made the bed, today.
I almost thought I was over you
.....for a minute.

I never lied to you.
I always told you the truth
            about love.
The joke is:
        You listened to me.
            I didn't.

Part Three

I crowed
What I knowed
Bestowed
What I knowed
You hoed
What I knowed
And growed
What I knowed
But I slowed
What I knowed
And stowed
What I knowed
Then you goed
Up the road
And I blowed
What I knowed.

I know myself ......
Now that you have left ....
        I shall be everywhere
          hoping to make such memories
            with someone else.
That is when I will really feel
        you have gone.

My body is suspended . . .
My mind is lost in space . . .
My tongue just wobbles loosely
                back and forth . .
Saying nothing . . .
Doing nothing . . . .
Out of time and out of place.
Like a bird . . . in dead of winter . . .
                flying north.

What were you . . . . .?
Who were you . . . . . .?
Something in me . . . . I know that.
       But you were like a drug.
While you were near,
       you were the ultimate "high".
With you . . . I could split atoms,
       stop time . . .
       stay young . . .
Or, I thought I could.
But you only gave out small doses of yourself,
       enough to keep me coming back.
And I could never be sure
       when you would be available again.
Soooo . . . . the inevitable crash . . . withdrawal!
I won't break windows, kill,
       or steal for a "fix" . . . .
but I sometimes feel I might die
       for need of you.

As with Tennis...
        never play "Love"
        with someone
        whose game
is not as good as yours.
You'll end up losing...
        and they won't
        know enough
        to care.

Without ever having you . . . .
    I have lost you.
Without ever knowing you . . . . .
    I know you . . . .
There is no history . . . .
    Only a memory
    that never occurred at all.
    A memory . . . .
    I can never forget.

It was a certain kind of sun, then . . . .
And dreams and hopes hung like thick smoke
                              in the air.
Lyrics of songs jumped out at me
                like playful kittens around
                                 a corner.
It is a long-remembered, half-forgotten time.
Where is it now?
Waiting for me . . . . or for you . . . somewhere?
Or has it gone its way . . .
                like the morning of your smile?

We weren't living together,
anyway.
We were hiding together.

"Pain and loneliness make you strong . . ."
  I dish that one out a lot!
Today, I don't want to be strong.
  I want to dream just as much
  as anybody else.
But, I keep on paying my dues, anyway,
  and I really don't want
            to belong
            to that club
                anymore.

You were so busy finding yourself
in me . . .
That I had to run from you
To keep you from killing
both of us.

Have you learned, yet,
That who you know
is not
who you are?

The softer I walk
The louder I hear.

To own anything
      is to be owned by it.
I never wanted to own you . . .
      it's impossible . . . .
and I never wanted to be owned.
But, I guess
      I always wanted you
      to pretend
      that you thought
      I was worth owning.

If all the "if's" and "maybe's",
"wish I were's" and
  "could have been's
  if only things
  were different
  than they are"
could fall right off a cliff . . . . .
Maybe I'd discover how
  to live with
  what is here and now . . . . .
but then,
I might as well forget this
  cause I started it
    with "if".

In those moments of despair . . .
            when I really don't care
            whether or not I survive,
then, am I most keenly aware
            of the certainty that I will.
                    That's the pain of it . . .
            and the miracle.

Part Four

I am astounded
　　at how long it takes
　　　　to discover . . .
　for the first time,
the things I have learned . . .
　　over and over again
　　　all my life.

The real growth
          is in recognizing
          that we *do*
          always get
what we want in life . . . .
          one way or another.

<u>Nobody</u>'s perfect!
   <u>Somebo</u>dy doesn't have to be.

Most loneliness
        is pain . . . .
peering into mirrors
        of self-pity
        with the hope
        of seeing someone else
                to blame it on.

Listen to what you criticize
                most severely
And you will hear
                what you most fear
                you are.

I was always afraid of
        risking *risk*.
But I found that I could stand
        to risk *risk*.
better than I could stand
        to fear *fear*.
At least, risking
        brought about changes...
and the changes took up so much time
I forgot what it was I was afraid
        to risk losing...
        in the first place.

The nicest thing about my life, now, is
that I am here with me
most of the time.

There is no such thing
          as perfect freedom . . . .
There is only the freedom to
          discover
          that there is
no such thing
          as perfect freedom!

It is much easier to be lonely
            without someone . . .
Than it is to be lonely
            with someone.

Real belief
is a quiet thing . . . .
too busy being itself
to look for disciples.

It is a waste of time and energy
    to worry about
        what others are thinking
            about you.

        because . . . .

You can never know
    exactly what another person
        is thinking . . . . . AND,
        the worst part is . . .
    they are not usually thinking
        about you at all.

They are too busy worrying about
    what others
        are thinking about them.

So, the truth is, all those terrible thoughts
    you thought they might
        be thinking about you,
    are your own thoughts
        about yourself.

Better spend your energy
    worrying about that . . . . or,
        you just might
        convince somebody to think
    what you were afraid
        they might be thinking
            after all.

It isn't always best
       to let everything
       spill out.
At times,
       there is more to be gained
       by using restraint!
Remember,
       it is the water
       held back by the dam
       that lights the city!

Always trying
        to be a good person
can be the biggest block
        to becoming one.

To live happily with a pet
one must, first, accept
the responsibility
of disciplining it
consistently and firmly
with much love!
To live happily with ourselves . . .
it is the same.

Who you are
     is not
     who you were . . .
It is who you are.

Any day of the week
I would choose to be "out"
    with others
    and in touch
    with myself . . . .
than to be "in" with others
    and out of touch
    with myself.

I can tell how secure I am, now.
I no longer clean the house
    the day before the maid comes!

Love is not a thing
        to be "in" or "out" of.
It just is.
The beginning is the ending . . . . .
the ending . . . the beginning . . .
Always and
        never . . . .
        forever.

In youth . . . .
        man seems to satisfy loneliness
             with passion . . . .

And in maturity . . . . .
        aloneness . . . . with compassion.

What a pity the difference
        is most often discovered
        after muscle and bone
        can no longer climb
            to the top
            of the mountain.

I have come to regard unrequited love
like a hole in the sock.
Mend it! or discard it!
Don't just stand there with cold feet!

Disciplining ones'self
        can be carried
        too far.
It is allright to relax
        part of the time.
Even the soil is richer
        when it rests
        every seven years.

If I keep talking about
        what I believe in . . .
Eventually . . . .
        I will tell myself
        how much I believe in
        what I talk about.

Since I've finally
      taken responsibility
      for my life—

I can't tell you how often
      I've wanted
      to give it back.

      But, nobody wants it.

      Isn't that lucky?

Good love is like good wine.
One can always remember the taste
of a Vintage year.
Wherever you are......
Salute!

Nothing matters, now.
I mean . . .
     everything matters so much
That nothing matters, now.

Alone can be beautiful.
It's the one truth
    we know to be certain.
    We are
    A Lone.
To embrace that truth
    is the first step
    to becoming
    Al One!

I walk down another street.

Aware and alive
>to the little I know,

>as if I've arrived
>at another plateau.

>A plateau...familiar...
>yet,
>wonderfully strange

>where I find my milieu
>in the fortunes of change.

In my soul is a room
>with a wedding inside...

>Alone
>is the groom
>and truth is
>the bride.

Pity has gone
>to its place on a shelf...

>to be summoned for others
>but,
>rarely for self.

>>Touching and feeling
>>in heart and in brain
>>Accepting the healing
>>of joy
>>that's in pain...

Where *Alone* is not gloom
>nor a fearsome divide.

>>Alone is the groom
>>and truth is
>>the bride.

Your alone-ness
        nourishes and protects
                my own.
        I am always on the watch
                for you.
No need to wear a carnation!
I'll know you . . . by me . . . .
                but you can hurry
                if you want to.